Birds That Live at the Water's Edge

Children's Science & Nature

BABY PROFESSOR

EDUCATION KIDS

What do you know
about water birds?

Have you seen them where you live?

Behold an
Amazing Sight!

Kids, in this book you
will get to know the
birds that live at the
water's edge. You
can see these birds
when you go for a
walk or have a picnic
near the seashore
or along rivers.

The water's edge is
an amazing place for
some birds. It is a rich
and busy place for
them. These birds nest
along the banks. The
shorelines and the
shallow waters are
their essential habitat.

Let's look closely as some of the water birds parade before us with their amazing characteristics.

What are water birds? Technically, these birds are called aquatic birds. They are the birds that live on or around bodies of salt or fresh water or in swamps or marshlands. Water birds have adapted to their environment. They live, nest and raise their young near and on the water.

Some of these birds have webbed feet, long bills for catching fish, and long legs for standing in deep water. Some of these birds can dive to catch their prey in water, and even "fly" underwater. Here are some of the wide variety of aquatic bird species.

Seabirds. Meet the marine birds. These birds are adaptive to life on the ocean and on large lakes.

The Graceful
Penguins. They
are considered as
the most aquatic
of all diving birds.
Penguins can dive
underwater but they
have to return to
the water surface
to breathe just like
marine mammals.
They mainly feed
on small shrimp
known as krill, but
some of them also
eat squid and fish.

Seagulls. They are also known as the garbage birds because they eat almost anything they can find. They are voracious eaters and tend to fight with each other over food. They will even eat dead animals. They are not afraid of humans. Some gulls live near the ocean but they are also capable of living near lakes far away from the sea.

The Fantastic Wading Birds. These are also known as diving birds or shore birds. These include flamingos, cranes, storks, egrets and herons. Sandpipers and plovers are smaller wading birds.

They occupy shallow-
water habitats.
Wading birds can
live both in fresh-
water and saltwater
shallow environments.
Their long, thin
legs allow them to
walk through water
easily. Interestingly,
they do this without
getting wet all
over their bodies.

They get their food in different ways. Some diving birds stir the water with their feet for food while others filter food using their beaks. In addition, larger wading species use their long legs and long necks to get at their food below the water's surface.

Get to know the Anseriformes. Anseriformes comprise about 180 living species of waterfowl. They are the ducks, geese, and swans.

Ducks. They belong
to the Anatidae bird
family and are mostly
aquatic birds that
can live in both fresh
water and salt water.
Their feathers are
highly waterproof,
so even if they dive
underwater their
under-layer feathers
stay completely
dry. Ducks feed on
small fish, insects,
and worms.

What are
freshwater birds?

Birds live near lakes
and rivers, wetlands,
and swamps. They
are often expert
divers and swimmers.
They include ducks,
herons, kingfishers,
and flamingos. They
are fun to watch, and
to hear. Birds like the
loon have distinctive,
haunting calls that
you may hear across
a lake at night.

The water birds have distinctive characteristics that make them unique. The flamingos, for example, appear pink because of the color of the food they eat. Storks are considered as symbols of good luck in many cultures.

Water birds enjoy living in their habitats. They deserve protection. Hence, human actions should not disturb the water birds' existence.

Did you enjoy reading? Share this to your friends.

Visit

BABY PROFESSOR
EDUCATION KIDS

www.BabyProfessorBooks.com
to download Free Baby Professor eBooks
and view our catalog of new and exciting
Children's Books